CW00406893

WHY WORRY!

The Christian's Vocation to Trust in God

by
William Lawson, SJ

*All booklets are published thanks to the
generous support of the members of the
Catholic Truth Society*

CATHOLIC TRUTH SOCIETY
PUBLISHERS TO THE HOLY SEE

CONTENTS

WHY WORRY!

Attitude and Character

Human beings, in their attitude to life, are either optimists or pessimists. There are innumerable shades of optimism, from the 'incurable' sort to the cautious and occasional: and pessimists range similarly from dwellers in unrelieved gloom to those who vary from light to shade like a landscape mottled with cloud-shadows.

It is, you may think, a matter of temperament. Your attitude to life depends on the character with which God endowed you. Perhaps He made you, fortunately for you, of the cheerful sort, enjoying the character that used to be called sanguine, full of the joy of living, much in demand for parties and picnics, brightening the lives of others by the freshness and joy of your manner and appearance. Without much effort, you bring happiness to yourself and others. Small credit to you, it is a gift of God.

And small blame to you, surely, if you are a
burden to yourself, and no help to others. Is it
your fault if, by character and temperament,
almost by nature, you look on the dark side of
things? You don't like being depressed. You are
depressed, and discouraged and disconsolate
because you can't help it.

I should like to convince you that you can
help it. No matter what your character may be,
there is never any need to be oppressed by life
and unequal to it. More than that, it is wrong to
be afraid of life, to lose courage, to think that
life is too much for you. Being a Christian, you
have a privilege and a duty of constant
happiness and steady courage. A Christian is, by
profession, cheerful, confident, peaceful, serene
and courageous.

Our Lord's Words

Does that statement need proof? The proof is in
the words of Our Lord in His Sermon on the
Mount. Notice that they are addressed, not just
to the Apostles as a summary of the ideal of

their high vocation, but also to an everyday crowd as an account of their elementary Christian duty. Listen to Our Lord's words:

'Do not be anxious. That is why I am telling you not to worry about your life and what you are to eat, nor about your body and how you are to clothe it. Surely life means more than food, and the body than clothing! Look at the birds in the sky. They do not sow or reap or gather into barns; yet your heavenly Father feeds them. Are you not worth much more than they are? Can any of you, for all his worrying, add one single cubit to his span of life? And why worry about clothing? Think of the flowers growing in the fields; they never have to work or spin; yet I assure you that not even Solomon in all his regalia was robed like one of these. Now if that is how God clothes the grass in the field which is there today and thrown into the furnace tomorrow, will he not much more look after you, you men of little faith? So do not worry; do not say, "What are we to eat? What are we to drink? How are we to be clothed?" It is the pagans who set their hearts on all these

things. Your heavenly Father knows you need
them all. Set your hearts on his kingdom first,
and on his righteousness, and all these other
things will be given you as well. So do not
worry about tomorrow: tomorrow will take care
of itself.' (*Mt 6:25-34*)

There you have a downright statement that
you must not worry, and then a few easy
questions, to underline the statement, about how
you compare in value with birds and flowers
which are so clearly provided for by God.
Finally there is a promise that, when you make
the kingdom of God the first object of your
concern, then God's Providence cares for you.

The Birds of the Air

It is worth your while to consider the examples
given by Our Lord. The birds of the air and the
flowers of the field are looked after by the
Providence of God. They sing and grow in
today's rain and sunshine: or they struggle to
find warmth in frost or moisture in drought.
They take the good and the bad in life as it
comes: and, having enjoyed a good day or

survived a bad day, they spend the night in
peace. The birds of the air, when they have
tucked their heads under their wings, do not
untuck them and remark to their neighbour or to
their own mind that last year's famine was
severe, and that the chances are there will be a
worse famine this year. They don't add the frost
and famines of yesterday, still less those of
tomorrow, to the hardships of today.

Do What You Can

You are to learn a lesson from those lesser
creatures of God. Imitation of their carefree
neglect of past and future must not be carried too
far. Since God has given you memory and fore-
sight, you must use them, recalling experience
and making it guide you in the future. It is your
duty, not only to look ahead and provide as best
you can for the future, but even to imagine
possible misfortunes so as to avoid them.

But, having used your God-given faculties
in that sensible way, having done all that lies
in your power, you are then, so our Lord says,
to be perfectly content, knowing that you have

done your best and that God will look after you. You may not, being a Christian, be anxious. In other words, you may not worry. What you can do, is what you have done. What you can't do is taken care of by the Providence of God.

Worry is Waste

Is that the way you practise Christianity? Or do you, when you have arrived at the limit of your powers of mind and body, settle down to worry about what you can't do? Do you distract and disturb yourself with excess of anxiety? Do you let yourself slump into depression and melancholy? Do you lose your courage, and tremble at the thought of what the future has, or may have, in store for you?

If you do that, then you are wasting your time and your energies. Is it the slightest use to puzzle your brain and nag at your mind over a problem that, by definition, you can't solve? You are troubling yourself about something which it is beyond your power to change or remove: and that is not sensible. In that same

Sermon on the Mount Our Lord asks a question which you can easily answer: 'Which of you by being anxious can add one cubit to his span of life?'

Will you, by worry, lengthen your life, improve your work, achieve professional or business success? Will you find money by worrying? Will you win security in body or soul, now or in the future, for yourself or for those you love? worrying is so much time and so much strength thrown away. It is as useless as:

'the toil of dropping buckets into empty wells, and growing old in drawing nothing up.'

Worry Does Harm

Not only do you gain nothing by that excess of concern which we call worry: you also lose by it. As the Book of Ecclesiasticus says: 'Sorrow has destroyed many, and there is no profit in it.'

Sadness, or depression, or discouragement may make you ill and shorten your life: but it pays no dividends. When you give your mind to the intense consideration of what is not your concern, when you go in fear of the future, when you add, to the reasonable labour of doing what you can do, the unreasonable toil of worrying about what you can't do, then you use, in beating the air, strength which you might have used to good purpose, and that strength is missing when you call upon it. As Ecclesiastes says (*2:22-23*): 'For what does he gain for all the toil and strain that he has undergone under the sun? What of all his laborious days, his cares of office, his restless nights? This, too, is vanity.'

Isn't it folly to wear out your mind during the day with over-anxiety, and then to lose your sleep in the same vain questionings? Yesterday's problems are no nearer solution: and you have no heart and no energy for even the ordinary problems of today.

Worry Rejects God's Help

There is yet a greater loss from worry. It loses you the special protection of God. You employ your powers to the full in an effort for the present and the future of yourself and those who depend on you. When you have done what you can, to distress yourself because of what you can't do is to poach on God's preserves, as though you could not trust Him to do His part. That is a kind of rejection, more or less deliberate, of His help. and He does not force His help on those unwilling to receive it.

'Woe to the listless heart that has no faith for such will have no protection.' (*Qo 2:13*)

But to rest tranquil and confident after you have done your insufficient best is to appeal for God's aid: and it will not be denied.

'A blessing on the man who puts his trust in the Lord,
    with the Lord for his hope.
    He is like a tree by the waterside
    that thrusts its roots to the stream:
    when the heat comes it feels no alarm,
    its foliage stays green;
    it has no worries in a year of drought,
    and never ceases to bear fruit.' (*Jr 17:7-8*).

Worry is Un-Christian

So far, the argument for trust in God instead of worry has been that confidence is the best policy. It pays. Confidence, moreover, is virtue: and worry is vice. There is no place for worry in a Christian life. Worry is un-Christian. It results from trying to bear the hardships of life without the support of Christian principles. I am far from saying that if only you will trust in God you will escape tribulation. No human being can go through life without sorrow and suffering. As Paul and Barnabas preached from the beginning: 'We all have to experience many hardships before we enter the kingdom of God.' (*Ac 14:22*).

It is part of the penalty of sin, and we can avoid it no more than we can avoid death. But there are two ways of taking those afflictions of body or mind or heart or soul. The bad way is to carry them alone, thinking that it is by your own unaided efforts that you are to bear the burden which you cannot escape.

Sorrow without Sadness

To do that is both unreasonable and un-Christian. And it makes you a prey to sadness. A Christian is not allowed to be sad - that is, to let his sorrow turn sour and bitter. Sorrowful you will certainly be if you have any human feeling: but you must have a 'godly grief' in St Paul's phrase.

'To suffer in God's way means changing for the better and leaves no regrets, but to suffer as the world knows suffering brings death.' (*2 Co 7:10*)

Our Lady is honoured by her title of Mother of Sorrows. But she was never sad, because she could not be selfish in her sorrow, nor could she let it turn her thoughts and her will from trust in God. That is the Christian ideal: and it should be yours. No matter what your anxiety, your fear, even your tragedy may be, you must face it, or bear it, in that Christian spirit. There is no exception to the rule requiring confidence in God.

'No harm can come to the virtuous man.' (*Pr 12:21*)

To be sad, or discouraged, or afraid, is to forfeit the most profound and universal experience of Christian life, that, no matter who you are, you are never alone and defenceless, that you are essentially, and all the time dependent on God, and that He supports you. To act as though you depended entirely on yourself is to be ignorant of elementary Christianity or to have obscured that elementary truth by your inflated notion of your own power and importance. To worry is a sign of ignorance or else of conceit and even of pride.

Never Out of Your Depth

You know very well that you can't manage everything in life on your own. You don't run your life. Life is a partnership between yourself and God. When you have done your best, you leave what remains to be done to Him - He is your partner. Live your life in that sensible and Christian way, and you can't be beaten. Nothing can take the heart out of you. You never get out of your depth.

Imagine someone swimming in the sea. While the surface is fairly smooth, he swims serenely enough. But when the waves begin to mount, swimming is not so easy. the swimmer grows agitated, and splashes desperately, increasing the size of the waves and draining his strength. He opens his mouth in fear to cry out, and swallows part of the sea. Perhaps he sinks and stays under. At best, he makes no progress in rough water: and when the calm follows, he is too weary and blown to do more than float exhausted. He is no help to himself, and he is a burden to others. That is a picture of the man who worries.

But the Christian, finding the waves too much for him, at once gets his feet down, and stands, head and shoulders above the waves, on the unchanging truth that he is in the care of God, and that, when he has God's help, nothing is too much for him. His troubles remain, but they are in proportion. They cease to loom over him, darkening his life. He stands above them, and can look across them at the goodness and the power of God.

Providence and Living by Faith

I do not say that trust in God lays bare to the Christian all the designs of God's Providence.

'It is hard enough to work out what is on earth,

laborious to know what lies within our reach;

who then can discover what is in the heavens?' (*Ws 9:16*)

Inevitably, the Providence of God is too much for our understanding. The human mind has a limited capacity. It can hold just so much and no more. How then could it possibly contain the plans of an infinite Providence? You must resign yourself to living by faith and not by sight. Once again, it would be a sign of ignorance or of pride to expect God's plans to coincide with yours. That truth you know, however much you may play with the idea of being your own Providence.

Given a free hand, you could remove the hardship from your life, and from the lives of those you love. To all for whom you are concerned, you would give plenty of material things, gifts of body and mind, success and security in their careers, and the real treasures of life - the riches of love and affection among family and friends. And, of course, you would provide for their spiritual welfare, ensuring their salvation. It would be comforting and satisfying to play Providence like that. But supposing you had to choose between that Providence of yours, which you understand so well just because it is the fruit of limited knowledge and limited goodness, and the Providence of God, founded on an exact and complete knowledge of every one of His creatures, planned with infinite wisdom and directed by a love for you and for all whom you love, which is at the same time personal to you and infinite, which one would you choose? Well, you have no need to make a choice. You are living now in that Providence of God, known perfectly to God as a person, cared for personally from moment to moment by the endless wisdom and endless love of God. So why worry!

'The Lord is my light and my salvation whom need I fear?

The Lord is the fortress of my life; of whom should I be afraid?' (*Ps 27:1*)

My Power is Made Perfect in Weakness

With that foundation, you can live always in serenity and peace, with your essential happiness out of reach of the trials and sorrows of life. You can even welcome evidence of your own weakness and insufficiency. By all human standards, you would say that the time to be confident, to be sure of your future, was when you had all the means necessary for success - all the material goods, all the strength of body and mind, all the support of human affection of which you felt in need. By Christian standards, which take account of the fact that you have a divine partner in life, you are confident not only when you are weak but because you are weak: for then there is more room in your life for your partner's work. That is what St Paul says:

'About this thing I have pleaded with the Lord three times for it to leave me, but he has said, "My grace is enough for you: my power is at its best in weakness." So I shall be very happy to make my weaknesses my special boast so that the power of Christ may stay over me, and that is why I am quite content with my weaknesses, and with insults, hardships, persecutions, and the agonies I go through for Christ's sake. For it is when I am weak that I am strong.' (*2 Co 12:9-10*)

That disposes, doesn't it, of your feeling that at the least sometimes you might be justified in losing courage? When everything has gone wrong, when not the thinnest ray of hope can cut through the clouds massed over your future, then surely you are allowed to droop and be sad. On the contrary, that is the time to look up, for rejoicing. That is the time for the power of God to be made perfect in your infirmity. You can't suppose that the power of God will be embarrassed by the difficulties which are too much for you. God's power is always infinite: and He uses that power out of endless love for you. Why worry!

Prayer and Serenity

St Paul summarises the Christian attitude to life in a sentence of the Letter to the Philippians: 'There is no need to worry; but if there is anything you need, pray for it, asking God for it with prayer and thanksgiving, and that peace of God, which is so much greater than we can understand, will guard your hearts and your thoughts in Christ Jesus.' (*Ph 4:6-7*)

Remember that your life is a partnership with God, and that you have the duty and the right to call on His power and His love in all your needs. Do what you can, using the gifts of God, to provide for yourself and for those who depend on you: and then leave the rest, confidently, to God.

That is the essential - to establish yourself firmly in the peace which belongs to the Christian soul, and to let nothing disturb your peace.

Courage in Fear

And if God chooses you for a hard Providence, remember that there are no exceptions to the command to be rooted in the peace of God. Your sorrows will come upon you; your character will keep its tendency to discouragement and depression; you will be afraid of the present and the future: but amid the

uncertainties of life, you will possess that
certainty of the immense love of God on which
your life is built, and your weakness will give
place to the perfection of the power of God.
Any coward can be brave when he is aflame
with courage. The Christian is courageous when
he is frightened to death: and his courage is
real, because it flows from the certainty of
God's Providence.

Cast All Your Cares Upon God

You will never fully understand the
Providence of God, not even when your trust
in God is perfect. God's choice of ways of life
and times of death may not coincide with
yours. Don't lose your peace and serenity and
courage in puzzling over what you cannot
understand. Recall your mind constantly, until
it is fixed in them, to the truths that you do
know - the omnipotence and the infinite
wisdom of God, and God's infinite love,
personal to you, which uses wisdom and
power to care for you and yours. Accept

humbly what you cannot understand. 'Bow down, then, before the power of God.'

But find, in your knowledge of God's goodness, the unshakeable peace and the endless courage which ensure your happiness now and forever.

'Unload all your worries on to him, since he is looking after you.' (*1 P 5:6-7*)

Informative Catholic Reading

We hope that you have enjoyed reading this booklet.

If you would like to find out more about CTS booklets - we'll send you our free information pack and catalogue.

Please send us your details:

Name ....

Address ....

....

....

Postcode ....

Telephone..

Email ....

Send to: CTS, 40-46 Harleyford Road,
            Vauxhall, London
            SE11 5AY

Tel: 020 7640 0042
Fax: 020 7640 0046
Email: info@cts-online.org.uk

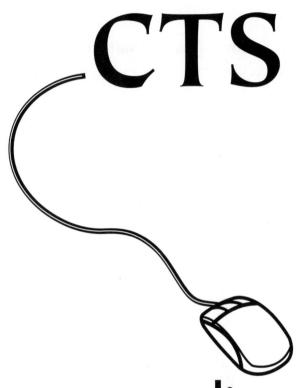

CTS

... now online
www.cts-online.org.uk